ILLUMIN

MW01137745

Secrets of the DRY BONES

THE MYSTERY OF A PROPHET'S VISION

Ezekiel 37:1–14

SUSAN ROHRER

Infinite
Arts
Media

SECRETS OF THE DRY BONES:
Ezekiel 37:1–14 - The Mystery of a Prophet's Vision
(Illuminated Bible Study Guides Series)
Written by Susan Rohrer

Kindly direct all professional inquiries to:
InfiniteArtsMgmt@gmail.com

Readers may contact author at:
facebook.com/SusanRohrerAuthor

All Scripture quotations taken from the New American Standard Bible®, Copyright ©1995 by The Lockman Foundation, used by permission. (www.Lockman.org)

Images are used under license from morgueFile.

Author photo by Adam DeBenedittis

Elements of the life story and work of William Cowper are drawn from the public domain.

ISBN-13: 978-1494336080
ISBN-10: 1494336081

Published in the United States of America

First Edition 2021

To every soul in bone-deep

need of resurrection

"*Behold, I tell you a mystery; we shall not all sleep, but we shall all be changed, in a moment, in the twinkling of an eye, at the last trumpet; for the trumpet will sound, and the dead will be raised imperishable, and we shall be changed. For this perishable must put on the imperishable, and this mortal must put on immortality...then will come about the saying that is written, 'Death is swallowed up in victory.'*"

I Corinthians 15:51–53, 54b

Contents

A Mysterious Way

"But we speak God's wisdom in a mystery, the hidden wisdom, which God predestined before the ages to our glory."

I Corinthians 2: 7

Tell the truth. When you look to the Bible for inspiration, are the images that come to mind as unsettling as this photo seems? No doubt, when you're searching for something uplifting to study, the last place you may want to linger is in some mysterious valley, littered with an entire army's worth of dry bones.

Ezekiel 37:1–14 might be one of those passages some tend to avoid. Many find it easier to tiptoe past pictures like this, in search of lighter, more self-explanatory fare. Then again, this graphic vision is recorded in God's Word. It's part of what the

Psalmist declared to be *a lamp to his feet and a light to his path.* That means the path through this ancient valley, no matter how mysterious it may seem, can be a source of revelation, restoration, and refreshment, even thousands of years later.

CASE IN POINT:
William Cowper

Even those who don't recognize William Cowper's name are probably familiar with his work. His often-misquoted eighteenth century hymn echoed the Apostle Paul as he observed: *"God moves in a mysterious way, His wonders to perform."* Certainly, William wrestled with his share of God's mysteries.

Did you know that this prolific hymnodist and forerunner of Romantic Poetry, this sensitive man whose works were admired by the likes of Coleridge and Wordsworth, waged a life-long battle with anxiety, depression, and doubt?

Just like many today, William Cowper was all too familiar with dry bones valleys. In fact, William became so spiritually dry that he made multiple suicide attempts. More than once, he descended into insanity.

A mysterious way, indeed.

You might ask: why would a man with such a romantic heart despair so profoundly of life? Early hardships shed light. Born to a devout household, after losing his beloved mother at the tender age of six, William was sent off to a boarding school where he became the victim of a cruel bully. Crippling insecurities took root.

Later, as a young law student living with his uncle, William fell in love. Her name was Theodora, and he longed to marry her. Poetry poured from the depths of young William's soul, but it was a union that was never to be. Theodora was, after all, William's cousin, too close in relation to be considered proper. Still, the break from Theodora was almost more wrenching than William's already drying bones could bear. God became even more of a mystery than ever to him.

How did William still come to write some of Christendom's most enduring hymns of praise? We'll follow more of his journey in later chapters. But William's life is a reminder that people come into these parched valleys step by step, just like he did. True stories like William's can help us put flesh and blood onto the dry bones passage we're about to study.

Through numerous applications you'll find in this book, we'll examine some of your stories, too.

These personal experiences can give fresh relevance to what might seem an arm's length text. As we investigate the mysteries of the Bible, these stories can help unlock the mysteries of our own hearts.

The Mystery of Mysteries

Ever stop to think: why does God speak in mysteries at all? That's a preliminary puzzle to solve. It's also a fair question to ask, especially of a God who invites us to reason with Him:

- *Why does the Bible speak in symbols, parables, and mysteries?*

- *What keeps even leaders and scholars from understanding God's mysterious ways?*

- *Will these mysteries ever be solved?*

Ponder these questions before you move on to Ezekiel's vision itself. Allow time for the Holy Spirit to speak to you and help you understand. Since we'll be studying a symbolic vision, it helps us to start by wrapping our heads around why God chooses to communicate with us in this veiled way.

If you're in a group, you can compare notes with others about possible answers to those questions. Cite leads from Scripture to corroborate your theories. Here are a few leads to get you started:

- Proverbs 25:2
- Mark 4:11
- Colossians 1:25–27

Look up these leads to see how each verse speaks to the corresponding question before it. See? At the heart of every mystery, there are lots of leads to run down and many clues from Scripture to be considered.

Sure enough, the Bible has its mysteries, but it also has plenty of tip offs, inspired by the Holy Spirit. They're there to help us solve even great conundrums.

Still wondering why God speaks in mysteries? Think about Jesus, how He taught the secrets of the kingdom in parables, stories of everyday people to whom His hearers could easily relate. While the casual hearer didn't understand, what happened with the disciples? The mystery engaged them to probe for more. And when the disciples earnestly sought Jesus for answers, He readily divulged each story's symbolic secrets.

Mysteries are like that. They capture our imaginations and stir our inquisitive minds to action. Symbolic visions like Ezekiel's dry bones valley are embedded with a message only those with ears to hear will come to understand.

Those lingering questions of ours actually do a good work. They prompt us to dig for explanations. Like hunger and thirst, they keep our attention itching till our curiosity is scratched with solutions.

We love to ferret out the clues, to follow and solve the mysteries we watch on television and movies, or read about in books. Think how great that *aha* feeling is when you figure out whodunit before your favorite detective does. How much more should we long to understand the sometimes-veiled truths of Scripture? Moreover, how much must our God appreciate the way mysteries draw us to seek Him out for answers?

Think of it. The Author of our faith actively longs for us to find the clues He's confided through the prophets. He wants us to investigate symbolic visions and dreams, like Ezekiel's vision of the dry bones. He waits for us to dig deep and unearth the secret treasures that those who seek Him are ultimately rewarded to discover.

The sharing of secrets is a privilege of intimate relationship. That's exactly the kind of closeness

God wants to have with His people. He will give us understanding of these mysteries when we sit at His feet. What is hidden will be brought to light. Understanding will grow as we get to know Him better, in that secret place of fellowship with Him.

Before We Venture Onward

I'm hoping you'll take a moment to pray before you read about Ezekiel's vision. It's amazing how much more fruitful reading the Bible can be if we first invite the Holy Spirit to come alongside us.

You can start off by acknowledging how much we all need His counsel whenever we study the Bible. You can add how dearly we appreciate it when He breathes life into what can seem like ancient dry bones. You can tell Him that you love it when He shows us great and mighty things we hadn't seen before, even after repeated readings.

My prayer as you embark on this study is that it will be an adventure in faith for you. They say that you really get to know a person when you travel side-by-side. So, invite the Holy Spirit to be your traveling companion and Teacher.

Exploring the Scriptures really can be a bit like investigating a mystery. So, grab your Bible, take His hand, and let's see what we can uncover to together about Ezekiel's dry bones vision.

The Case File:
Ezekiel 37:1–14

"The word of the LORD came expressly to Ezekiel the priest, son of Buzi, in the land of the Chaldeans by the river Chebar; and there the hand of the Lord came upon him."

Ezekiel 1:3

At the beginning of every mystery, detectives open a case file. Pertinent data is drawn from history. Present day evidence is gathered for study, in the hope that it will lead to a solution.

Our case: Ezekiel's enduringly fascinating vision, the valley of the dry bones.

The case file is recorded in the text of Ezekiel, a priest. Let's start by reading the entire text of

Ezekiel's dry bones vision from the Bible. If you're in a group, you may want to ask someone to read it aloud. Carefully absorb the scene, picturing each element, as if following a mystery.

Below is God's Word, recorded by Ezekiel:

"The hand of the LORD was upon me, and He brought me out by the Spirit of the LORD, and set me down in the middle of the valley; and it was full of bones.

2 And He caused me to pass among them round about, and behold, there were very many on the surface of the valley; and, lo, they were very dry.

3 And He said to me, Son of man, can these bones live? And I answered, "O Lord GOD, Thou knowest."

4 Again He said to me, "Prophesy over these bones, and say to them, 'O dry bones, hear the word of the LORD.'

5 Thus says the Lord GOD to these bones, 'Behold, I will cause breath to enter you that you may come to life.

6 And I will put sinews on you, make flesh grow back on you, cover you with skin, and put breath in you that you may come alive; and you will know that I am the LORD.' "

7 So, I prophesied as I was commanded; and as I prophesied, there was a noise, and behold, a rattling; and the bones came together, bone to its bone.

8 And I looked, and behold, sinews were on them, and flesh grew, and skin covered them; but there was no breath in them.

9 Then He said to me, "Prophesy to the breath, prophesy, son of man, and say to the breath, 'Thus says the Lord GOD, Come from the four winds, O breath, and breathe on these slain, that they come to life.' "

10 So, I prophesied as He commanded me, and the breath came into them, and they came to life, and stood on their feet, an exceedingly great army.

11 Then He said to me, "Son of man, these bones are the whole house of Israel; behold, they say, 'Our bones are dried up, and our hope has perished. We are completely cut off.'

12 Therefore prophesy, and say to them, 'Thus says the Lord GOD: Behold, I will open your graves, and cause you to come up out of your graves, My people; and I will bring you into the land of Israel.

13 Then you will know that I am the LORD, when I have opened your graves, and caused you to come up out of your graves, My people.

14 And I will put My Spirit within you, and you will come to life, and I will place you in your own land. Then you will know that I, the LORD, have spoken and done it, declares the LORD.' "

Ezekiel 37:1–14, NASB

Quite a powerful vision, isn't it?

In fact, this vision is so monumental that we tend to stand back and look at it from afar, instead of considering the depth of its relevance to our own lives today. That's why this study will guide you through numerous personal applications. We'll call them "BONE SCANS" since they're geared at giving us a look inside our spiritual lives.

Ready to take a closer look?

BONE SCAN:
Casting this Mystery

Now that the biblical text is fresh in your mind, imagine that a live-action mystery movie is being made. This picture would depict Ezekiel's dry bones vision in vivid detail. It would boast an enormous cast with roles for all applicants.

We won't presume to cast the role of the Almighty. But here's a basic cast list of available human roles, as they appear in stages, along with their developing character traits:

CAST LIST

Ezekiel – (Leading Role) Despite years of persecution, he still keeps his eyes and ears alert to what God would show him. Determined and devout, yet humble, he's an often outspoken leader, outcast from worldly social circles. He hangs on God's every word, and is surprisingly commanding when he hears it. (In accordance with Joel 2:28–29, both men and women can be considered for this role.)

Dry Bones – Thoroughly parched, they feel oddly disconnected with the massive crowd of God's people. They have no eyes or ears to perceive their Maker. Closer inspection reveals breaks that tell of many past trials and scars that hint at debilitating shame. Deep down, they realize how cut off they are, but they've lost all hope of doing anything about it. (Must be able to cry on cue.)

Inert Bodies – Able to lie prone for extended periods of time, they have most of the elements of life. They're in the process of being restored, but they're still oddly stationary. They are present among God's people, but there's no breath in their nostrils. They're not yet functioning as vital members of the body of Christ. At this stage, they are easy prey for predators. (No experience necessary.)

Live Soldiers – (Supporting Roles) Standing erect in the ranks of God's people, they steadily draw in the breath of life. Their faces shine with promise.

They remain on high alert to receive marching orders from their appointed leaders. They're an active part of an exceedingly great army, equipped and advancing in power. (Must be able to take direction well.)

Got it? There are four roles we're typecasting. Not one of God's people will be left uncast. Now, reflect upon your current spiritual life experience. Take a little time to look inside yourself to honestly answer these questions:

- *Which of these four roles would I most closely identify with playing at present?*

- *Which roles have I played at some time in the past?*

Allow a few moments to think about your personal situation. Be realistic. Resist the urge to think of how you'd cast anyone else. Just think of which role suits you the best, exactly the way you function spiritually at this point in your life.

Once you've typecast yourself, go back to the cast list anew. Forget typecasting yourself in the role closest to who you are or have been. Ask yourself:

- *If I could take on the role of my dreams, which role would it be?*

Write down the answers to these three questions. If you're in a group, you might take a few minutes to compare notes. You may find that there are those who feel as if they've played three or four of these roles at one time or another. You might also ask for a simple show of hands from those who have been through a season of spiritual dryness or inactivity. (Don't be surprised if almost every hand gets raised.)

Take some time to consider the differences between those Inert Bodies and the Live Soldiers. Remember, it doesn't matter how many committees we serve on or how many programs we populate if we're not moving in the vitality of the Spirit. The flesh on those Inert Bodies may give them the appearance of life within church circles, but in order to take our places in the truly alive ranks, we need the Holy Spirit to breathe on us in power.

Ready to investigate Ezekiel's vision? Let's keep this perspective toward personal application in mind as we delve deeper into our mystery.

Notes & Inspiration

Scene of the Crime

"The hand of the LORD was upon me, and He brought me out by the Spirit of the LORD, and set me down in the middle of the valley; and it was full of bones. And He caused me to pass among them round about: and, behold, there were very many on the surface of the valley; and, lo, they were very dry."

Ezekiel 37:1–2

If you've watched any amount of crime shows on TV, you know the drill. The detective gets a call. He or she is summoned to the crime scene. No matter what else has been going on at that moment, the detective drops it and rushes to the scene, while it's fresh. The investigation begins with a thorough scouring of the physical location.

Did you ever wonder why detectives use flashlights when entering a crime scene instead of just turning on the lights? They do that to focus their attention more closely on one element at a time. Try reading Ezekiel's verses with a flashlight or a magnifying glass and you'll see what I mean. It causes you to concentrate more fully on what you might have otherwise missed. That's how closely we want to look at how the dry bones passage applies to our lives.

Put yourself in Ezekiel's sandals as this vision begins. Imagine that God has placed a hand on your shoulder. He guides you to the place where a massive crime has taken place. It's not a singular homicide in this case. He brings you to a valley that is literally filled with dry bones. You are not kept on the sidelines. Instead, the Spirit sets you down, right in the middle of this shocking scene.

What do you notice?

Take a moment to observe for yourself before you move on with the study. Check Ezekiel's text. Think about the specifics of the scene. Make notes.

If you're studying this case with a group, consult with others. Mention everything you observe that has bearing on this investigation. To get you started, ask yourself this question:✗

- *Did these people die of natural causes or is this a crime scene? Cite a verse in the text to corroborate your answer.*

Once you think you've spotted everything, move on to see some of what I've drawn from Ezekiel's text:

- *We're looking at the scene of a crime, a mass murder. These people didn't die of natural causes. They were slain (v. 9).*

- *This is not a fresh crime scene. The fact that no flesh remains and the bones are so dry tells us it's a very cold case. They've been dead quite a while (v. 1).*

- *Since they have no flesh or sinews, the bones must be disconnected from each other. Otherwise, why would they come together in verse 7? The victims' testimony confirms that they are "completely cut off" (v. 11).*

- *The bones are out in the open. It's as if either no one has discovered them or has cared enough to tend to the remains (v. 2).*

- *The scene where this mass murder or suicide took place is a valley (v. 1).*

Let's focus on just the setting first. With all of those bones, it would be easy to overlook the physical surroundings where this crime took place: in a valley.

Down in the Valley

Think about it. As much as we love the mountaintops of life, more often than not, life sets us down in a low place, an arid valley where we are vulnerable and exposed to attack. Here's what happens:

- We feel cut off from others.
- We lose a sense of ourselves.
- We're too blue to pray.
- Our wells run dry.
- Hope perishes.

Have you ever been in that kind of valley? William Cowper certainly had.

CASE IN POINT:
William Cowper (continued)

No matter how improper William's romance with his cousin was deemed, anyone who has suffered a severed relationship can understand something of the resulting trough of depression where William found himself. Suddenly, he was cut off from his loved one. He was alone, vulnerable, and quite heartbroken. He was also still grieving the loss of his mother. Insecurities reemerged. Hope perished, and with it, William's mental health.

In time, William recovered via treatment at an asylum under the care of a Christian doctor. It was there, while studying the book of Romans, that William put his faith in Jesus.

Once released, William found acceptance in Christian community. He was taken in by a retired minister and his wife, Mary Unwin. An older woman, Mary helped nurse William back to stability.

Around this time, perhaps as a means of encouragement, John Newton invited William to add to a book of hymns he was putting together. Of the

348 *Olney Hymns* (including Newton's *Amazing Grace*), William contributed lyrics for sixty-some hymns, a number of which are still popular today. Among them was his composition, *Light Shining out of Darkness*, which opens with what is perhaps his most familiar line, about the mysterious way in which God works.

Even as a believer, like Jacob of the Bible, William continued to wrestle with God over the deep mysteries of faith. It was nearly his undoing.

As evidenced by William's poetry and many spiritual songs, great art was birthed out of great pain, even what became an unhealthy preoccupation with the enigmas of death, atonement, and salvation. This fixation would come to get the better of William as the strain of preparing for examination by the British House of Lords brought on three suicide attempts, the last of which was nearly successful.

Already in his young life, William had suffered several major triggers for depression and anxiety: the early loss of a parent, abandonment from his home, the bullied destruction of his confidence, romantic heartbreak, and the dashing of his professional aspirations. Each time, his bones got drier.

At some time or another in our lives we, too, may find ourselves in these dry bones valleys. We get separated from our friends and other loved ones.

Loss and disappointment lead to discouragement and despair. Spiritual vitality drains. The cares of this world choke the breath right out of us. We're parched by draining circumstances.

CASE IN POINT: My Dry Bones Valley

Just so you won't think I've been exempt from this kind of thing, here's a snapshot of a trek I took through a challenging season.

In early 2008, I passed through the valley of the shadow of death. Literally. It began in January with the unexpected passing of a dear friend. As confident as I was about her eternal security, it seemed like I'd never stop mourning. I missed her so much.

In March, I learned that my father—a believer whom I adored beyond expression—had been given just a few months to live. We had also begun to lose our mother to that long goodbye, a little at a time. My siblings and I set much of our lives aside to care for our mom while our dad attempted the long-shot treatment that became his ultimate demise. Before or since, I've never seen anything like the way he suffered and died.

Days later, my father-in-law passed, but that was not the end of this season of grief. Within two weeks' time, there were four funerals in my family, all unrelated passings, one right after another.

As it was with me, sometimes these valleys we come upon are situational. In time, the shadow passes. We find refreshment in the wellspring of the Holy Spirit. He breathes on our dry bones, and with His help, we move through that difficult season.

But there are those, like William Cowper, who find themselves languishing in the shadow of death. They are the flesh and blood residents of the valley of the dry bones. It is for their sake, and for the sake of all God's people, who suffer from spiritual dryness at one time or another, that we continue to investigate the scene of this crime. We persist, no matter where it takes place—even if it's perpetrated in the recesses of our own hearts.

BONE SCAN:
Location, Location, Location

Are you starting to think about where you are right now, in your life? This part of the exercise is not intended as a measure of your relationship with God. Everyone goes through hard times. Even Jesus spent a lot of time in the wilderness. God can give us streams in the desert. For now, just think purely about your life circumstances, like how your relational, professional, and home life are going.

Make a simple line drawing of two mountains with a wide, flat valley in between. Got it? Where would you draw your circumstances into that picture? (Different categories—like family, finances, health—can be marked in different places.)

Ask yourself:

- *Am I ascending the foothills?*

- *Am I on top of a mountain?*

- *Do I feel myself falling from heights I once enjoyed?*

- *Am I camping out in the valley?*

Okay. No matter where you located yourself on a circumstantial level, answer these questions:

- *Am I happy right where I am?*

- *Do I wish I were somewhere other than where I am?*

- *Would I fear a change from my present location?*

Here's the thing. On their own, our physical circumstances don't tell us much about what's going on inside us, spiritually. Our circumstances can have us celebrating the peaks, when our spirits are as dry as a bone. Remember what those altars God kept asking Israel to tear down were called? High places.

> *"When I had brought them into the land which I swore to give them, then they saw every high hill and every leafy tree, and they offered there their sacrifices...then I said to them, 'What is the high place to which you go?' "*
>
> Ezekiel 20:28 – 29a

When we read such references, something inside us breathes a sigh of relief. We know that we don't build literal altars or offer sacrifices on them anymore. We think we're off the hook, at least on this count.

The problem is, we forget just how quickly we erect idols of the heart. We rationalize how much we sacrifice for these oft-attended passions. We forget what God had already spoken through the prophet, Ezekiel.

"Any man of the house of Israel who sets up his **idols in his heart***, puts right before his face the stumbling block of his iniquity."*

Ezekiel 14:4

So, let's not confuse our circumstantial position with our spiritual condition. Let's boldly look where others don't. Let's examine those things we've exalted in our hearts, those things that cause us to stumble into sins like pride, greed, lust, and covetousness.

When it comes right down to it, the most tempting time to neglect our relationship with God can be when things are going great. We have so much fun celebrating our highs that we forget the One who gave us what we wanted so much in the first place. We turn that blessing into a curse.

We push God aside. We rationalize or ignore His warnings. We go our own way. We don't drink from the well of His Spirit. Dry bones, here we come. And if our bones dried on our peaks, what will happen in our valleys? (See Luke 23:31.)

On a spiritual level, valleys can actually be wildly underrated. There are times when the valleys of our lives can be our sweetest times of communion. There is rich marrow. There is life in our bones. Streams spring up in that desert (Isaiah 48:21).

✗The Apostle Paul talked about learning the secret of flourishing in the circumstantial valleys of life. Take a look at what he wrote from prison:

> *"Not that I speak from want; for I have learned to be content in whatever circumstances I am. I know how to get along with humble means, and I also know how to live in prosperity; in any and every circumstance I have learned the secret of being filled and going hungry, both of having abundance and suffering need. I can do all things through Him who strengthens me."*
>
> Philippians 4:11–13

It's interesting to notice that there's no physical description whatsoever of the valley floor itself in Ezekiel's vision. It's the bones he talks about in such detail.

A valley can be a lush, fruitful place as long as we are watered by the Holy Spirit. We can be like those trees Ezekiel talks about, in the valley below the cliffs of Engedi. Year-round, we can bear fruit if we're drinking from God's river (Ezekiel 47:12).

Ever notice how the Bible has a way of turning conventional wisdom completely on its head? Highs can masquerade as criminal lows. Lows can be the acmes of spiritual growth.

So, friends, when it comes to finding godly contentment, it's not so much a question of *where* we are as it is *who* has led us to that place. If God led you into that valley, thank Him for it. He will strengthen you to not only survive it, but also to thrive. Wherever you are, there is a Fountain. Truly.

But—and this is a big caveat I'm about to float out here—if it wasn't God who led you to that place you're in, if you followed your fleshy heart's desire there, you may have made yourself vulnerable to crimes of a cataclysmic spiritual dimension. That can leave your spirit victimized. It can mean spiritual dryness, even death.

That's how it was for the Israelites in Ezekiel's dry bones valley. That's how it can be for any of us who ignore God's voice of warning.

It's not like God stood idly by as His people wandered into their doom in that perilous valley. Repeatedly, He warned them that their dead bodies would be found there, around the altars of their idols (Ezekiel 6:5).

The problem was, they refused to listen. They wanted what they wanted. Those high place idols became more important to them than their relationship with God. The results were both comprehensive and catastrophic. They became the victims of a crime, every one of them. ✗

BONE SCAN:
True Motives

Wherever you located yourself, mountaintop or valley, let's examine any motives that may have drawn you there. If you're suffering in a circumstance that you had no part in choosing, then consider your motives for that circumstance pure. But if you had any control over a spiritually draining position you're in, ask yourself these questions:

- *What brought me to the scene of this crime?*

- *Which behaviors of mine keep me here?*

- *Am I dying at the altars of any idols of the heart?*

- *What high places do I need to tear down?*

- *Have I asked God to help me tear down this idol of the heart? If so, have I any ignored warnings and course corrections He's already given me?*

- *What practical steps can I take to leave this spiritually drying circumstance?*

The Promised Homeland

No matter the place you find yourself, know that God sees you there. Like the loving Father that He is, He cares about your mountaintops and your valleys. Wherever you are, you are never, ever, out of His sight. He waits to water your dry bones and to restore you to a place of spiritual vitality in every single circumstance.

Still, you may notice in Ezekiel 37:12–14, the vision bears a promise. Look there for God's response to the dry bones' cries of hopelessness. A change of location is foretold. God promises to release them and bring them into their own land.

Imagine how encouraging this promise must have been to Israel, given the physical captivity they were suffering in Babylon. What hope this promise of release and return must have instilled in their downtrodden, homesick hearts!

As with all of God's promises, the hope that He raised did not disappoint. There was a literal fulfillment via the restoration of Israel's earthly homeland, but there's also a far-reaching, figurative aspect to this promise. It extends to all generations of God's people, to Jews and Gentiles alike.

Wherever we may be situated in this life, we can find comfort in God's promise that a heavenly homeland awaits. The best really is yet to be. Earthly dwelling places come and go, but our heavenly home is eternal. Those who have entrusted their lives to Jesus are already citizens of this everlasting kingdom, a place especially prepared for us (John 14:2).

When we reach the gates of that Promised Land, it will not be like entering a foreign country. Entry isn't earned. Jesus bought our passports at the price of His own blood. It's a matter of going home.

As we find ourselves in difficult places here, we must fix our eyes on this eternal hope:

> *"For our citizenship is in heaven, from which also we eagerly wait for a Savior, the Lord Jesus Christ."*
>
> Philippians 3:20

This is the secret that helped Paul to find bone-deep contentment as he wrote to the Philippians, while chained up and in prison. He knew that he was heir to a great overriding hope, a promise we should all cling to despite our dry bones valleys.

Feeling hopeless? Having a hard time feeling at home in that valley? Take heart. This world is not our home. Heaven is. Forever. What a bright and glorious hope Christ freely gives, to all who would dare to believe.

Notes & Inspiration

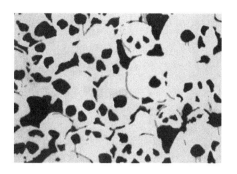

Whodunit?

"The thief comes only to steal, and kill, and destroy; I came that they might have life, and might have it abundantly."

John 10:10

Doubtless, a horrendous crime has been perpetrated against humanity in Ezekiel's valley of dry bones. Such acts cannot go unpunished.

The burning question that hangs over every crime scene is: whodunit? Authorities ferret out clues, searching for someone to blame. The guilty must be brought to justice. Suspects are identified. Repeat offenders are interrogated.

Imagine that you've been deputized in this case. It's time to round up suspects.

A valley is filled with the bones of the slain before you. Ask yourself:

- *When spiritual dryness and death occur, who exactly is to blame?*

- *What thief has stolen away the abundant life that all of God's people were meant to live?*

The Apostle Paul leaves us a clue to the culprit in these crimes against God's people:

> *"For our struggle is not against flesh and blood, but against the rulers, against the powers, against the world forces of this darkness, against the spiritual forces of wickedness in the heavenly places."*

> Ephesians 6:12

The Apostle Peter echoes a caution to all who would underestimate the danger of this plot against the household of God.

> *"Be sober of spirit, be on the alert. Your adversary, the devil, prowls about like a roaring lion, seeking someone to devour."*

> I Peter 5:8

Yikes. We're looking at a massive plot, serial spiritual terrorism, and danger arising seemingly out of nowhere. Looks like it's a culprit that Jesus has already dealt with in His own valley of temptation (Luke 4:1–13).

When Jesus explains the parable of the soils, He gives us a lead in this case. He tells the disciples plainly who it is that "*snatches away*" the good seed that has been sprouted in a person's heart. He's clear about who sows the tares that can choke the life out of a growing believer.

Whodunit? Jesus clearly fingers the perpetrator in Matthew 13:38–39:

> *"...the tares are the sons of the evil one; and the enemy who sowed them is the devil."*

Jesus knows this culprit's M.O. It is the enemy himself, the accuser of the brethren.

In earthly investigations, once a potential culprit has been identified, tell me. What is the first thing that authorities do? They label him or her as a "person of interest." They check the suspect's history. They print up a rap sheet.

A quick check reveals that this particular suspect of ours has a very long list of priors. Jesus testifies against him:

"He was a murderer from the beginning, and does not stand in the truth, because there is no truth in him. Whenever he speaks a lie, he speaks from his own nature; for he is a liar, and the father of lies."

John 8:44

A thief, a killer, and a destroyer, all from the very beginning. From his first appearance in the Garden of Eden, that snake's endgame is our destruction. Interrogate him and all he'll do is lie, since after all, he initiated the practice of deceit.

He's honed his craft for thousands of years. He knows just how to trick us, how to lure his unsuspecting prey into his deadly snare. He'll fabricate excuses. He'll say he wasn't there. And do you know what his biggest con of all is? He'll try to convince us that he doesn't exist. Then he'll point the finger back at us, in merciless accusation.

⚔ CASE IN POINT:
William Cowper (continued)

Remember William Cowper and those repeated suicide attempts? In his depression-ridden state, William had a terrible dream. When he awoke, he fell prey to the enemy's suggestion that this dream meant that life was over for him. He became convinced that he had already perished and was doomed for all eternity.

Sadly, William was tortured by the mistaken belief that this dream was from God, and that, through it, God was telling him to end his life. But it wasn't God at all. Instead, the perpetrator was the enemy, taking the opportunity to trick William into prematurely ending the life God had given him.

The Blame Game

So, we've identified the culprit in our valley of the dry bones investigation. Just like with William Cowper, the devil is to blame. Only this time he's killed off the entire house of Israel. Cuff and convict. Case closed. Right?

Not necessarily.

The devil is one culprit, sure. But stop. Think about it.

- *Did the enemy act alone?*
- *Could it have been a conspiracy?*

Dig for clues that suggest a pattern in the case of our old brother Job. Remember, though God allowed the enemy to take just about everything else, God did not allow him to take Job's life. Job could have been tempted to do that himself, when even his wife suggested that he curse God and die. Instead, Job clung to God for his life, despite it all.

In the midst of his suffering, four voices vied for Job's attention. These same voices called out to William. They speak to us today in the blistering heat of our dry bones valleys: ✗

1. **The voice of the enemy** that discourages, disparages, accuses, and sows doubt. This lying voice tempts spiritual and physical suicide. He's a serial kidnapper, luring us away from our Father God's presence;

2. **The voice of human reasoning** that draws us out of the flow of the Spirit and into fleshy logic. It's the voice of self-reliance, not faith;

3. **The voice of our own desires** that suggests sin will satisfy us. Desire gives way to lust and idolatry. Sin dries our bones, and causes a lingering death by attrition;

4. **The voice of the Holy Spirit** who urges us to silence the other voices and to choose abundant life with God. While the other voices clamor for our attention, the Spirit often speaks in still, small whispers.

All the way from Eden to the present day, whenever there is spiritual death or dryness—let alone an entire valley of dry bones—these same four voices continue to speak.

Admittedly, the enemy of our souls plays a dastardly role. Yes, other people can lead us astray, into dark and dry places. But perhaps the most powerful of the first three voices is the voice of our own desires. Ironically, though this voice originates from within our own hearts, it's the culprit we most often overlook. It's also the voice to which we most readily listen.

We may point our fingers at others. We may bluster that "*the devil made me do it.*" But dryness of spirit will persist until we take ownership of the ways that we, ourselves, are at fault.

From the case of Ezekiel's dry bones to the contemporary deadness of our own spirits, we must realize when we're complicit in the enemy's schemes. We must allow the Holy Spirit to do that work of conviction that we steadily resist. We must allow Him to regenerate us, to breathe new life into us.

Sure enough, there are times when we've done nothing wrong to bring about an attack from the enemy. We aren't always to blame. But in more cases than we may care to admit, we've abetted the enemy's crimes against us.

When the Bible says *"we wrestle not with flesh and blood"* it's very clear that our enemy doesn't act alone in his crimes against us. The enemy might initiate, but it takes at least two to make up a spiritual wrestling match. The enemy always engages a human partner. It may be someone else.

But it also might be you.

It wasn't God who tempted William Cowper to take his own life. The devil wasn't the only one to blame. Sure, other people colluded. But ultimately, it was a despairing William who strung the rope.

James makes our part in the sin that can cause spiritual death and dryness clear in his Epistle:

> *"Let no one say when he is tempted, 'I am being tempted by God'; for God cannot be tempted by evil, and He Himself does not tempt anyone. But each one is tempted when he is carried away and enticed by his own lust."*
>
> James 1:13–14

Often, what we're looking at is, in fact, a conspiracy. In our human frailty, simple desire grows into full-blown lust. That thing we want so much becomes an idol. We collude with the enemy. We allow ourselves to be carried away from God's life-giving River. We are enticed away from the safety of His presence, only to be driven into the exposed, waterless valley of our demise.

BONE SCAN:
Dusting for Prints

I've yet to meet anyone who actually wanted to have fingerprints taken, even when that person has done nothing wrong. There's something so personal, so identifying of what we've put our hands to doing.

Just like a fingerprint, sin puts distinctive marks on our spirits. They are deadly blots we all leave on everything we touch. Try as we might, we can't erase them on our own. Only God can wipe these prints from our lives. The good news is, He's all too willing to do it—if we sincerely ask.

Naturally, we resist this kind of thing. It can be downright scary. But once a problem area has been identified, we can ask God to help us attend to it. So, let's get brave and dust for our own prints. Let's see what might not be so visible to the naked eye. Ask yourself:

- *What specific sins have I put my hands to lately?*

- *Are there things that go through my mind that I'm glad I can keep secret?*

- *How have I contributed to my spiritual dryness?*

Stop. Really ponder this for a while. Make note of anything that comes to mind. What desires of the flesh, what idols of the heart have attracted us to this place?

This exercise is not for the purpose of heaping condemnation on ourselves or upon each other. It's about honestly investigating the sometimes hidden truths of how we've allowed the enemy to draw us away from God's lush garden, to cut us off from the Spirit's life-giving waters, and to victimize us in this dry valley.

Our complicity isn't easy to look at, much less to dwell upon for long. We're quick to defend ourselves. We reflexively sputter out alibis. Yet, we stand guilty, all of us, in desperate need of a Savior.

In the privacy of your thoughts, take some time with this exercise. Bravely investigate the state of your spirit. Know that frightened heart of yours is likely to resist arrest. It may run, desperate to evade apprehension. Bear down and pursue the truth, even if it's difficult to capture.

Admittedly, it won't seem as intriguing to examine how we may have abetted the enemy in his crimes against us. But the spiritual stakes could not be higher. Until we face up and get to the bottom of this with God, that deadly dryness will persist. Since our very lives are at risk, it's a mystery well worth solving.

Once you've noted all your fingerprints, just look at all the promises God sets before you, the minute you turn yourself in, and over to His mercy and grace:

- **Deliverance** – Psalm 18:17–18 ✗
- **Protection** – Psalm 61:3
- **Restoration** – I Kings 8:33–34
- **Redemption** – Psalm 106:10; 107:2–6
- **Triumph** – Psalm 41:11

✗ Always remember: no matter whodunit, no matter how devastating the circumstances, your Father in heaven longs for the return of every prodigal, from the runaway spendthrifts to the ones who stayed at home and died on the vine.

We may feel like we've blown it for good, like we're unlovable messes, but forever and always, God is for us, longing for the day when we turn from our own ways and head for the comforts of home.

"I have set before you life and death, the blessing and the curse: therefore choose life that you may live, you and your children."
Deuteronomy 30:19 ✗

Notes & Inspiration

Forensic Evidence

"Now faith is the assurance of things hoped for,
the conviction of things not seen. For by it the
men of old gained approval...And without faith,
it is impossible to please Him, for he who comes
to God must believe that He is, and that He is a
rewarder of those who seek Him."

Hebrews 11:1–2, 6

When it comes to life's great enigmas, theories abound. But when the stakes are as high as eternal life and death, guesswork shouldn't carry the day.

What we need is conviction. We need that know-that-you-know sense of what the truth really is. We need that sweet fruit of the Spirit:

Faith.

In most mysteries, hard evidence only takes us so far. We must search our hearts and decide what we believe is the truth. Since life or death sentences can hang in the balance, we connect the dots the best we can, searching for that soul-satisfying assurance about what remains unseen, beyond all reasonable doubt. We take that proverbial leap of faith. It's true in relationship with God and it's true as we examine the vision He gave to Ezekiel, this valley strewn with dry bones.

When it comes to dealing with capital crime, we know what investigators need, in order to secure a conviction. The solving of every such case demands compelling evidence. The scene is scoured. Physical and circumstantial pieces of the puzzle are gathered. An autopsy and labs are done. In and of themselves, these jagged bits might not look like much, but as they come together, a picture emerges.

BONE SCAN:
Inspecting the Evidence

Let's revisit the scene of Ezekiel's vision of that valley, filled with the dry bones of the entire house of Israel. Scan back through the vision. Look closely at those bones scattered across the valley floor.

Don't overlook the obvious, especially as we probe into the mysteries of our own hearts through personal applications along the way. Take some time with these questions. Here we go.

What do you notice about the bones in Ezekiel's vision?

Make note of your observations. Keep an open ear to what the Holy Spirit may show you, and what the significance of any observation may be. Notice:

1) **There are a lot of bones** (v. 1).
   This valley is literally "full" of bones, it says, enough to comprise an "exceedingly great army" (v. 10). The scope of this crime is staggeringly comprehensive. There are no survivors. The whole house of Israel, all of God's people are dead (v. 11). Ask yourself:

   - *How do God's people fall prey in such numbers?*

   - *How can I avoid following the crowd into dryness?*

2) **The bones aren't buried** (v. 2).
   They are abandoned, openly strewn "*on the surface of the valley.*" They are exposed to the

elements. For a Jew, this sight would have been particularly unsettling. That's because Jewish tradition encourages that bodies be buried as soon as possible, sometimes the same day a person died. For bones to remain unburied is considered disrespectful, a shame among the house of Israel. Ask yourself:

- *Have I left my life open to lethal elements?*

- *How do I avoid tending to my spiritual needs?*

- *Is there anything I do that, if uncovered, would bring shame to me or the body of Christ?*

3) **The bones are very dry** (v. 2).
They have been picked clean by predators and have become brittle. We can gather from this that they have been there for some time, baking in the sun. Ask yourself:

- *Do I feel spiritually dry?*

- *How do I contribute to my dryness?*

- *How do I make myself vulnerable to temptation or drying circumstances?*

4) There's no flesh on the bones.

These bones have no physical protection of any kind, nor any internal organs with which to function. They have no life in them (v. 6). Ask yourself:

- *What do I do to tend to the health of my spirit?*

- *How much time do I devote to spiritual cleansing, grooming, and clothing?*

- *What is my spiritual temperature? Is my spirit cold, lukewarm, warm, or hot?*

5) They're disconnected (v. 6–7).

There are no sinews to hold the various bones together. The fact that they must come together tells us that they are scattered apart. Ask yourself:

- *Am I in regular fellowship with a body of believers?*

- *Do I bear the burdens of others like I do my own?*

- *Am I meaningfully connected to other believers on a one-on-one level? If not, what can do to cultivate spiritually nurturing relationships?*

Tales the Bones Tell

As soon as we take the time to listen, we find out the truth: dead men *do* tell tales. Their stories are as heartrending and unique as the people who relate them. Yet, most have one thing in common: at some point and for one reason or another, they became disconnected from the people of God.

Whether they scattered of their own accord or were cast out from the rest of the body, the result is the same: spiritual dryness.

The antidote? Return and reconnect. Drink of God's life-giving Spirit. Fellowship with His people. Allow God to water you with the Word. Ask to be refreshed and refilled.

It may not seem as simple as that, but in fact, it can be. If you're the one feeling dry there really are things you can do about it. If you're not feeling dry, then take on the ministry of Jesus and help water the ones who are. These words from Hebrews give us a clue how to start:

> "*Let us draw near with a sincere heart in full assurance of faith, having our hearts sprinkled from an evil conscience, and our body washed with pure water...And let us consider how to stimulate one another to love and good deeds, not*

forsaking our own assembling together, as is the habit of some, but exhorting one another, all the more, as you see the day drawing near."

Hebrews 10:22, 24–25

Draw near.

It's an open invitation to this come-as-you-are party. We all need the cleansing stream Jesus offers. We all need the love of our brothers and sisters to encourage us toward revival. We all need to be washed in the pure water of His Spirit.

Where do we find this water? Look here for a clue:

"And he showed me a river of the water of life, clear as crystal, coming from the throne of God and of the Lamb."

Revelation 22:1

There it is, that refreshing River, flowing from the very throne of God. If you're feeling dry, just like the woman at the well, you need the wellspring of the Spirit. Drink of that water and you needn't ever be parched again.

"But whoever drinks of the water that I shall give him shall never thirst; but the water that I

shall give him shall become in him a well of water springing up to eternal life."

John 4:14

You see, disconnection from the Holy Spirit and those parts of the body flowing in His River brings spiritual dryness and death. Whereas, drinking in and flowing with the River of God brings life.

When you're in that current of the Holy Spirit, there will be plenty of evidence. His refreshing waters will overflow the confines of your being and splash onto other people. You'll bear fruit in and out of season, on the mountaintops and in the valleys.

If you or your group would like to learn more about the Person and works of the Holy Spirit, I invite you to read another *Illuminated Bible Study Guide*, an in-depth book I've written on that subject. It's called: *THE HOLY SPIRIT: Amazing Power for Everyday People.* I hope it will be an encouragement to you in your relationship with the Holy Spirit and in cultivating the spiritual gifts He has for you.

Bottom line, it really is all about relationship. It's about discovering true love and refreshment, in the arms of the Lover of our souls.

Notes & Inspiration

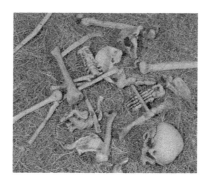

Witness Testimony

"...Every fact is to be confirmed by the testimony of two or three witnesses."

II Corinthians 13:1

Have you ever been called for jury duty?

Once, when I was being considered as a potential juror in a homicide case, I was asked if I would be able to vote *guilty* based solely on the testimony of one credible eyewitness. If the defendant were convicted, the prosecutor would seek the death penalty.

I had listened as, one by one, everyone ahead of me in the jury pool answered "yes" to this same question. What should I say? The Holy Spirit brought two verses to mind—Deuteronomy 17:6

and II Corinthians 13:1. God used the Bible itself to give me a confirmed answer.

Confirming Witnesses

Why isn't a single credible eyewitness enough in a capital case? Think how many death row cases have been overturned because DNA evidence later discredited single eyewitness testimony. As sincere as a person may seem, even a credible eyewitness can be sincerely wrong.

Especially when the stakes are this high, the Bible says that we need confirming testimony. Whether that confirming testimony comes in the form of evidence, character or personal witnesses, we need to make what we believe more certain by seeking out multiple witnesses.

So it is when we examine any manifestation of prophecy, like Ezekiel's vision.

So it is when we seek confirmation about whatever we sense God may be saying to us.

And so it will be as we call our first witness in the mystery of the dry bones.

This first witness will be asked to speak to the demise of the house of Israel in this valley. We call the Prophet, himself. He will give testimony through his biblical account, about exactly what he sensed, saw, and heard.

Ezekiel, the Prophet

When a witness steps into the box, one of the first questions asked is: "*What is your relationship to the deceased?*" Answers give context to the witness's testimony. They can either establish or erode credibility.

Inspired with 48 chapters of the Old Testament, there is much to be gleaned about the reliability of Ezekiel's account. A quick background check reveals that he had already accurately prophesied the fall of Jerusalem as well as their Babylonian captivity. Likely known by both Jeremiah and Daniel, Ezekiel had a long history of relating God's messages, even when they were wholly unpopular with or unflattering to God's oft-idolatrous flock. Ezekiel's name literally means *God strengthens*, in keeping with his ministry.

In addition to serving as a priest, more than once, God sovereignly appointed Ezekiel as a watchman over His people. Check out Ezekiel 3:17 and 33:7.

Serving as a watchman over a single person, let alone the entire house of Israel, was a sacred responsibility. If Ezekiel had neglected his watch by failing to deliver God's message of warning, he'd been told that the blood of the entire house of Israel would have been on his hands. So, over the course of more than twenty years, Ezekiel maintained this sober stakeout over Israel. He warned, corrected, and undergirded them with God's messages.

Across the generations, God still moves on the hearts of men and women to serve as prophets, priests, and watchers over His people.

CASE IN POINT:
Mary Unwin, Watchman

Remember William Cowper? Mary Unwin faithfully watched over William from the moment she and her husband took him in, long beyond her husband's passing, and for the rest of her life. Given the complexities of William's struggle for stability, it was neither an easy nor a short-lived assignment.

William's emotional health was never strong. He and Mary never wed. Still, the fact that she had no spousal obligation didn't deter Mary from answering God's challenging call. This devout widow faithfully ministered to and kept watch over William, as long as the Lord gave her breath.

We may think that this type of "watchman" appointment is only for leaders, or maybe pastor's wives like Mary Unwin. But Paul exhorts that everyone who has been reconciled with God has, in turn, been given the ministry of reconciliation. We have all been given the sacred responsibility to watch over one another, and to call the wandering home (II Corinthians 5:18–20).

Case in Point:
Ezekiel, Watchman

In his day, Ezekiel kept a long watch over Israel. He didn't do it because there was something in it for him. He stood in the gap, in the unfashionable ranks of the rest of the prophets of God—persecuted, largely ignored, and wildly unappreciated.

Still, Ezekiel selflessly recorded whatever God spoke and showed to him. He persisted out of respect for his relationship with God and out of faithful adherence to his sacred appointment as a watchman.

Actually, Ezekiel 34—37 show a turn in the type of revelation God gave through the Prophet. We begin to see messages of revival and hope. There are promises of God to feed and restore His people.

There was the assurance of deliverance through a coming Servant Shepherd. Renewed blessing and fruitfulness were prophesied. The indwelling Spirit would be given. But no matter the message—difficult or encouraging—Ezekiel reliably delivered.

BONE SCAN:
Reliability of Your Testimony

So, Ezekiel is Ezekiel. Nobody expects to be called on by the Lord on the scale that he was. No one expects to be called as a watchman.

Or should we?

What if the Lord did call upon you to speak to His people? What if the Almighty subpoenaed your testimony?

Consider the following questions:

- *Would my testimony as a believer be credible under close scrutiny?*

- *What would thorough examination of my conversations, writings, and life practices reveal about my relationship with God?*

- *Would I be willing to serve as a watchman?*

- *Have I ever been called upon to serve as a watchman over someone else? If so, what steps have I taken to carry out that responsibility?*

Okay. Say you look pretty good on paper. Your track record is squeaky clean. Look deeper:

- *Can I be relied upon to tell the truth, even when it's difficult?*

- *Am I hesitant to speak to others about my relationship with God and what He shows me?*

- *Do I let peer pressure intimidate me?*

What do all of these personal questions have to do with Ezekiel?

Everything.

Ezekiel was a human being, living in society, just like we are. He may have lived thousands of years ago, but he was subject to the same type of internal pressures we feel today. He had to deal with each of these questions, every time God asked him to serve as a mouthpiece for Him.

Now, let's look at another witness in this case.

The Witness of the Father

As the dry bones passage opened, Ezekiel testified that "*the hand of the* LORD" was upon him (v. 1). Ezekiel wanted his readers to know that this vision was not a figment of his imagination. This was not some random hallucination or dream. Ezekiel used his first words about this vision to let us know that he received it while he was under the initiating touch of his Father, God.

I'm no Ezekiel. I'm just an everyday believer who has made herself available to God. But, years ago, I received a night vision in which the right hand of the Lord was first placed on my right arm, then came to rest, warm and loving, just below my throat. Words fail to adequately describe this profound experience, but as I read Ezekiel's account, the assurance of how God leads us with His tender yet powerful hand, was as unmistakable as it was palpable.

Think about how frequently God confirms Himself by leading and ministering to us with His right hand (Isaiah 41:10). The Scriptures abound with confirming testimony, tracking with Ezekiel's witness.

Granted, God's hand is always there to help us, even when we don't physically feel it. But in this case, Ezekiel was so convinced that God's hand was upon him that he started off by positioning his testimony in that light. In so doing, he acknowledged God as the initiator of this vision. Ezekiel may have been holding the quill, but he wanted to be sure his readers knew Who really authored the words he recorded.

BONE SCAN:
Leading of the Witness

Have you ever sensed the Father's hand of guidance? If so, make note of a specific occasion. Now, ask yourself:

- *Do I discern God's hand readily, even when I don't physically feel it?*

- *Am I responsive to His touch in all areas of my life? If not, in what specific areas do I resist Him most? Why?*

- *What can I do to invite God's guidance?*

Ezekiel wasn't the only person God ever led in this very personal way, by hand. He's still leading us by His strong right hand, even today. The question is: will we take His lead? Do we invite His leading, or do we presume to take the lead ourselves?

Just how do we sense God's leading? Let's call on Ezekiel's next witness.

The Witness of the Spirit

Ezekiel goes on to recount that God brought him out to that valley of dry bones "*by the Spirit.*" So, it's implicit in Ezekiel's testimony that there was yet another compelling witness present: the Holy Spirit.

Confirming testimony is still given to believers by the witness of the Holy Spirit to this day. Jesus said:

> "*When the Helper comes, whom I will send to you from the Father, that is the Spirit of truth, who proceeds from the Father, He will bear witness of Me, and you will bear witness also, because you have been with me from the beginning.*"
>
> John 15:26–27

That's why our hearts still burn within us when we hear His voice. Hebrews 12:29 refers to our God as "*a consuming fire.*" When that fire burns in us, we can't help but be warmed, just as Ezekiel must have been. Jesus came to baptize us with the Holy Spirit and fire, so that as we sense the warmth of that holy blaze, we are empowered to testify for Him. We're assured of our standing with God to do that.

Among other verses, Romans 8:16 mentions this amazing dynamic:

"*The Spirit Himself bears witness with our spirits that we are the children of God.*"

Known as the Spirit of truth, He gifts us with discernment about the trustworthiness of other witnesses. Though often discounted, the witness of the Holy Spirit, testifying in our hearts, should be an important consideration in every case.

Also, the fact that Ezekiel said that the Spirit transported him into the center of this vision is of no small significance. Through this action, God demonstrated that He isn't a distant bystander when His people are perishing, even when it's their fault.

The Bible says that God is near, that He is in the midst of us. That is precisely where Ezekiel was brought: smack into the middle of the scene. There, the Holy Spirit stood ready to manifest in another way, as the breath of God, a Mighty Wind.

BONE SCAN:
Catching the Wind

Sensing the Holy Spirit's direction can seem easier said than done, huh? It's like Jesus said in John 3:8. We may hear the sound of that Wind, but we're not always so sure which way the Wind is blowing. It can be hard to distinguish His voice from our own, let alone the enemy's. Ask yourself:

- *Do I know what it means to be led by the Holy Spirit? If so, describe an experience.*

- *Do I take time to invite the Holy Spirit's presence? If not, how can I do that?*

- *Do I seek the confirming witnesses of Scripture about how I feel led?*

- *Have I asked the Holy Spirit to breathe on me in power lately?*

Maybe you've already been filled with the breath of the Holy Spirit. Perhaps you know what it is to be baptized in fire. Still, as life presses us, it's easy to get spiritually dehydrated. When that happens, it's all the more encouraging that the Spirit is a Fountain.

Isn't it wonderful that there's no limit to the refills we can receive (John 3:34)? Just like Paul encouraged the Ephesians, we can invite the Holy Spirit to refill us to overflowing, every step along the way. We need nothing less when we're called upon to serve those who are like Ezekiel's next witnesses.

The Witness of the Dead

Technically, this is hearsay testimony, but the Spirit giving witness is to be considered completely faithful and true. Look at His report of the voices crying out in testimony. Listen to how the dead speak:

> *Then He said to me, "Son of man, these bones are the whole house of Israel; behold, they say, 'Our bones are dried up, and our hope has perished. We are completely cut off.'"*
>
> Ezekiel 37:11

Can't you hear the desperation in their voices? They cry out from the desolate valley floor. They wail that their bones are dried up; their hope has already perished. They feel completely cut off from the wellspring of God's rejuvenating River, the company of His abiding love.

BONE SCAN:
Victim Testimony

If you've never been in a dry place, if you've never been tempted to give up hope, bless you. And tuck some tissues into your pocket, because sooner or later, if you live long enough, you're likely to visit this place. You may even set up camp and stay for a while. God will use even those hard times to help build empathy in you. He will equip you to comfort others with the same comfort He gives you (II Corinthians 1:6).

If you've ever been through a dry valley, like most of us, ask yourself these questions:

- *Was the dry valley an unavoidable life circumstance? If not, in what ways am I responsible for the resulting dryness I felt?*

- *What steps can I take to avoid spiritual dryness, even in trying circumstances?*

- *When I feel dry and discouraged, who do I call upon first for help?*

If you were honest enough to admit that God wasn't first on your call list, know you are far from alone. It's our tendency as human beings to reflexively reach out to humans we think will sympathize with us first. Still, how much better off we'd be if we made calling on our Father God our number one priority.

The reason we don't call on God first is that we don't comprehend what a loving parent He is. We doubt His goodness. We fear correction. We cower, forgetting how very forgiving He is. Look how responsive God was to Israel, even though it was their own rebellion that was killing them.

BONE SCAN:
Role Reversal

Remember in that opening BONE SCAN when we cast ourselves in Ezekiel's dry bones mystery, considering each of the human roles? Now, for the sake of empathy with our Father's heart, imagine yourself in His role as our divine parent.

Stop and listen to Israel's cries again, as if you are standing in the middle of Ezekiel's valley of dry bones, hearing their pleas, crying out all around you, for the very first time.

Now, think of how you would feel if all of these cries were coming from your very own children.

Loving them as you do, how would you, as a parent, feel?

Imagine yourself as the parent of an entire nation of prodigals. You've seen them as they grew from eager childhood to rebellious adolescence and into drying adult challenges. You advanced them a rich inheritance they'd done nothing whatsoever to earn. They've arrogantly squandered it. They've thrown your treasures at the feet of idols that only take and never give.

Now, your children find themselves destitute. They've wandered from home into this desolate valley. There is no food or water. They starve. They thirst. Right in front of your pooling eyes.

You recall how faithful you've been to them, even as they've gone their own way. Circumstantial evidence corroborates with history to indicate the odds-on probability. Rescue these prodigals and they will likely soon forget your goodness. They'll revert to their pattern of rebellion.

Still, your parent's heart watches for any glimmer, even the tiniest indication that they want to come home. Their cries ring in your ears. The voices of your dying children pierce into your side.

As hard as the carnage is to watch, your faithful nature refuses to let you turn from the awful scene. You know for a fact that no one else can save them.

You are, quite simply, their only hope—their Savior, the hope of Israel. Compassion wells within your heart.

Once again, you reach out to them. You send a star witness to testify on your behalf. All your children have to do is open themselves to receive the breath of life you offer them.

The Star Witness

In the case of Ezekiel's dry bones, we see that there were multiple witnesses, tracking with the Bible's directive. But who is our mystery's star witness? Exactly what is that star witness's testimony? There's a clue in the First Epistle of the Apostle John:

> "*And it is the Spirit who bears witness, because the Spirit is the truth. For there are three that bear witness, the Spirit and the water and the blood; and the three are in agreement. If we receive the witness of men, the witness of God is greater; for the witness of God is this, that He has borne witness concerning His Son...and the witness is this, that God has given us eternal life, and this life is in His Son.*"

I John 5:7–9, 11

Like John wrote, we may weigh the witness of human beings, but we should always give much more credence and consideration to the greatest witness of all: the witness of God concerning the gift of eternal life available through His Son.

You may ask: What does a prophetic vision from the Old Testament have to do with what John is talking about in his New Testament Epistle? Does Ezekiel's vision hearken in any way to the testimony of Jesus? Consider what we're told about the vital principle of prophecy in Revelation 19:10:

"For the testimony of Jesus is the spirit of prophecy."

So, prophecy, at its essence, is the testimony of Jesus. True, some of Ezekiel's prophecies found a measure of fulfillment on a literal, earthly level. But let's not forget about the farther-reaching, figurative dimension that prophecy is purposed to reveal.

Think of all prophecy as being an expression of that River of living water Jesus spoke of: the Holy Spirit. Ultimately, at the center of that River, the prophetic current flows in witness to the testimony of Jesus (Luke 24:27). That's why, even though Jesus isn't mentioned by name, we can still look for Messianic foreshadowing in Ezekiel's vision.

Just think how Jesus fulfilled the Father's promises as you read Ezekiel's text:

"Thus says the Lord GOD, 'Behold, I will open your graves and cause you to come up out of your graves, My people...And I will put my Spirit within you, and you will come to life...then you will know that I, the LORD, have spoken and done it."

Ezekiel 37:12, 14

This greatest witness of God, about the promise of resurrected life through His Son, overarches the Scriptures. Those who have eyes to see get glimpses of it all the way from Genesis to Revelation. Yes, Ezekiel's vision rings with the spirit of prophecy, the testimony of Jesus. The vision of the valley of the dry bones resonates with the coming of the Messiah and a lifesaving, eternal New Covenant.

Long after Ezekiel recorded his vision, the pledge of renewed life would continue to resound across the centuries. It would come to fulfillment by means of a stunning demonstration.

Just as in Ezekiel's vision, God loved us so much that He sent His Son to come into the midst of us. He came while we were those dry bones—dead in our sin, cut off and hopeless—in our valley of rebellion. When Jesus died and rose for us, He paid the ransom to open our graves. He breathed the breath of the Holy Spirit upon us and gave us new life. He did this so a world's worth of dry bones could find the hope of resurrection, once and for all.

That is why Jesus is called the hope of Israel. It's just as the prophets foretold. He is our Savior in the midst of every dry valley. He continues to call us out of our graves. He longs to revive us by His Spirit, and to bear glorious, confirming testament to God's abundant mercy and grace.

He is always and forever our mystery's bright and morning star witness, the greatest witness of all.

BONE SCAN:
Your Testimony

Suppose you have been called upon by heaven's highest court. You know they have your entire life on record—every word, every act, every secret idol of your heart—ready to replay at a moment's notice. There'd be no point in embellishing or understating the facts. You would be asked to tell the truth, the whole truth, and nothing but the truth.

Immerse yourself in this scene, as if it were really happening. Imagine you've been sitting in the courtroom, waiting. Finally, you are called by name. You rise and cross to the witness box.

- *Does anything about giving your testimony in public give you heart palpitations? If so, think about the reasons why.*

- *Are there any questions that, if put to you, would make you want to take the Fifth Amendment?*

You are asked to testify about any relationship you may have with Jesus. Make note of your answers to the following questions:

- *If you know Jesus personally, what is your history? How, when, and under what circumstances did you first meet?*

- *How would you briefly describe your present relationship, if any? (Would you call yourself a secret admirer or an open devotee?) Write down several short descriptors.*

- *If Jesus were called upon to bear witness, what role would He say you are playing in Ezekiel's dry bones vision today?*

Notes & Inspiration

Identify the Bodies

Then He said to me, "Son of man, these bones are the whole house of Israel; behold, they say, 'Our bones are dried up, and our hope has perished. We are completely cut off.'"

Ezekiel 37:11

Look closely at the church wall pictured above. Though, at first glance, they may look like stones on that wall, close inspection reveals the ironic truth.

It's hard to believe it, but those walls are covered with skulls and dry bones. At one time, these were all living, breathing, flesh and blood humans. Now, they cover the structure of this church. Who were these people and what brought them to this place?

The state of the remains seems to leave little to go on in the investigation of Ezekiel's dry bones. That centuries-old quote says that *dead men tell no tales*, but modern medical examiners and forensic pathologists beg to differ. Even long dry bones can speak volumes. They can tell of the wounds they have suffered, how they came to wither and die in this desolate place.

Victim Verifications

In the course of working a crime scene, perhaps there is no aspect more emotionally charged than the process of identifying a body. When it's a loved one who has been slain, it's all the more heartrending to confirm.

It's been said that there is no greater grief than what a parent feels over the loss of a child. Think of the agony a parent must suffer when it comes time to confirm the identity of his or her son or daughter.

How brave must we all be in these circumstances, when we're brought face-to-face with such tragedy? But gather our courage, we must, if we are to solve this crime, and with great respect to the slain, to bring the perpetrator to justice.

Take another look at that valley of dry bones, scattered all around you. Verse 11 holds a clue to their identity.

Who are the slain?

In verse 11, the slain are positively identified as "*the whole house of Israel.*" Let that sink in for a moment.

In this valley, our Father God had been bereaved of His entire household. He has brought us to the scene where every child—both natural children and those who were grafted into His family by adoption—has been brutally annihilated.

Think how His heart must break as He surveys the tragic scene around you. He recognizes each and every person represented there by name. He has known us from conception (Psalm 139). We are family. This couldn't be more personal to Him.

Every set of remains in that valley represents a real child, with real struggles, to our Father. Not a single soul escapes His notice. He has watched, heartbroken, as each one, in his or her way, has wandered into this depressed, vulnerable place. He has grieved as each has lost hope, and without the life-giving breath of the Holy Spirit, has perished. That the death they've succumbed to is spiritual only compounds His grief.

Identify with God's Heart

Think how hard it was for God, in His great love, to look upon William Cowper as his hope perished to the point of suicide, not just once, but multiple times. In His grace and mercy, God sent a watchman to come upon William, before it was too late. Still, He sees countless others push away help and perish.

Remember: the slain in Ezekiel's valley of dry bones are the entire household of God. That means this crime is personal for us, too.

We know the slain.

We are the slain.

Within the ranks of the church, we are more inclined to think of the unchurched as being the ones who are spiritually dead. We forget the scope of the problem within those who would seem the most devout. As Jesus observed, things are not always as they appear, even among church hierarchies:

"Woe to you, scribes and Pharisees, hypocrites! For you are like whitewashed tombs which on the outside appear beautiful, but inside they are full of dead men's bones and all uncleanness."

Matthew 23:27

Imagine how difficult it was for those religious leaders to hear Jesus' warning. Ultimately, it was a warning given in love. Jesus spoke out of concern for their spiritual welfare, and out of a desire that they'd receive Him and be resurrected.

As hard as it is, like Jesus, we must identify the bodies. We must be brave enough to come upon them in their dryness and despair. We must cut them down from their ropes, and help them to choose the life that God has set before them.

We must start with ourselves.

BONE SCAN: Personal Hydration

Take some time to honestly scan your own bones for a moment. Ask yourself:

- *Do I ever feel that I'm dry or even dead spiritually?*

- *Do I sense the refreshment of the Holy Spirit on a regular basis?*

Picture your life in the Spirit as a water glass. How much water do you sense in your glass right now? Is it:

- *Bone dry?*
- *Getting low?*
- *Half way?*
- *Almost full?*
- *To the brim?*
- *Overflowing?*

If you're anywhere shy of overflowing, know that God waits to pour out more of His Spirit on you. It's a free gift for every child of His who sincerely asks. (How do I know that? Just look at this clue: Luke 11:13.) And no matter how low your water supply may be, no matter how dry your bones, consider the promise of this verse:

> *"...I have set before you life and death, the blessing and the curse. So choose life in order that you may live, you and your descendants..."*
>
> Deuteronomy 30:19

Yes, God wants you and your descendants to live. We all need His living water to do that. This choice between spiritual life and death is set before His entire household. That includes every man and woman. That includes you.

In the privacy of your heart, ask yourself:

- *Am I reluctant to ask Him to refill me?*

- *Have I wandered from intimacy with God?*

- *Do I feel disconnected from close fellowship with other believers?*

- *Do I battle anxiety, despair, or depression?*

- *Have I lost hope that I'll see God's goodness in the land of the living?*

- *Have I considered suicide?*

- *Is it hard for me to admit my "yes" answers to any of these questions?*

Secrets of the Dry Bones

What are the deepest, darkest secrets of the dry bones? They are the true answers to those questions. They are the struggles we all try our best to hide— from each other, from ourselves, even from God. They are the hidden heartaches and the private practices that sap the life right out of us. They're the secrets we'd rather take to our graves than have the humility to admit.

Left hidden, these secrets can prove lethal. But if we can find the courage to come clean and ask for help from God and from each other, a miracle can happen. Resurrection can take place.

Amidst the Broken

In Ezekiel's day, there were very strict laws concerning dealing with the dead. When it came to the diseased and spiritually broken, the general practice was to stay away. Ostracize. With that in mind, take another look at where the Spirit of the Lord set Ezekiel down in verse one: *in the middle* of this valley of dry bones. The Lord placed Ezekiel strategically, in the midst of broken and dead people.

CASE IN POINT:
Coming Alongside

Many years ago, when I was just a teenager, I remember a friend of mine got into trouble with the authorities. Word quickly spread. Parents curtailed friendships. After all, this girl could be a bad influence on their kids.

My parents were very protective of me, so when my mother heard about this, I fully expected her to discourage me from associating with this girl, like other parents had. Instead, my mom surprised me.

I believe that my mother was following the prompting of the Holy Spirit when she encouraged me to make a point to seek out that girl, to be the kind of friend she needed in the midst of her troubles.

Other believers came alongside her, too. It wasn't long before Jesus rescued that girl and changed her life completely.

Isn't that just like Jesus—to reach out to the troubled, the sick, and the disenfranchised? I just love that about Him.

CASE IN POINT:
Jesus in the Midst

It seems that the minute Jesus entered a place, He did the exact opposite of what we tend to do. Instead of seeking out the most powerful, beautiful, influential, interesting, or safe people, He deliberately sought out the dry bones, the people no one else wanted to even be seen with in public. He sought out the diseased, damaged, disenfranchised, and even those thought of as dangerous.

When Jesus quoted the opening verse of Isaiah 61 in the temple, up front, He established the purposes of His ministry. He stood right in the midst of the house of Israel, the dry bones of Ezekiel's vision. Jesus said He was there to *"bind up the brokenhearted."* As His followers, we continue that ministry to the spiritually vulnerable, afflicted, and dead among us.

Just as Jesus advised in the parable of the Good Samaritan, stopping to bind up the wounded is the right thing to do. The sharing of personal stories often reveals brokenness of one kind or another. Think how much it pleases God when we set aside our own concerns to help tend to the wounds of others.

In the same way the human immune system was created with white blood cells to defend our bodies against harm, we should come alongside those who need undergirding and defense from harmful attacks or wounds they experience.

Like Jesus, we should:

- *"Bring good news to the afflicted."*
- *"Proclaim liberty to the captives."*
- *"Comfort those who mourn."*

It's not that we're supposed to put some clichéd bandage on the surface of a suffering person's complex problems. Sometimes in-depth professional counseling or treatment is needed outside group settings. What we can do in the moment is listen without judgment. We can care. We can wrap our arms around the person. We can say, "I love you," and mean it. We can find ways to follow-up with that person.

Ministry within group settings can be as unique as every need, but in general, the exhortation of Deuteronomy to *"choose life"* is followed by three practical ways that we can all encourage the broken to do that. Take a look at this verse and try to spot those three things:

> *"...by loving the LORD your God, by obeying His voice, and by holding fast to Him; for this is your life and the length of your days..."*
>
> Deuteronomy 30:20

Consider these leads for each of Deuteronomy 30:20's three exhortations:

1) **Love God** – Deuteronomy 6:5
2) **Obey His voice** – Jeremiah 11:2–4
3) **Cling to Him** – Proverbs 4:13

All three of these directives focus the broken person directly upon God. They invite new intimacy in relationship with Him. They foster growing in dependency on God Himself to guide, heal, and restore. They bypass an unhealthy dependence upon other people and encourage the person into the supportive arms of their Father.

Remember, it is not God's desire that we suffer in spiritual dryness or death. He doesn't want any of His people to feel cut off or beyond hope. Hebrew 7:25 says Jesus *"always lives to make intercession"* for us.

Think of it:

You are never beyond His concern

You are always on Jesus' prayer list.

Jesus is constantly talking to the Father on your behalf, advocating for you, knowing your every need. His desire is always to embrace us in His tender compassion, to bind up our broken hearts, to water our dry bones with His Word, to restore the very breath of His Spirit into our lungs, and to resurrect us to the glories of abundant life.

Those who follow Jesus should endeavor to do no less for one another. We should identify the dry bones in our midst. Then, just as Ezekiel was commanded to prophesy to the Breath, we need to entreat the Holy Spirit to breathe on the dry bones among us. We should take the time to pray for them, to reach out to them just like Jesus did—with understanding, forgiveness, and sacrificial love.

Notes & Inspiration

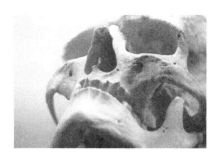

The Secret to Resurrection

And He said to me, "Son of man, can these bones live?" And I answered, "O Lord God, Thou knowest."

Ezekiel 37:3

"Can these bones live?"

When you think about it, this might seem like a startling question in context. Gazing around at a valley filled with dry bones, it must have looked patently obvious to Ezekiel that life was long over on a genocidal scale. If ever he'd seen a hopeless case, this was it.

Still, God saw fit to put this fascinating question to His prophet.

Imagine what must have run through Ezekiel's mind as he scanned the overwhelming scene. How should he answer God's question? If he said, "*No, the bones can't live*," would it be a denial of God's power, since God can do anything?

It looks like God asked Ezekiel a pretty tough question, doesn't it? The Almighty's capability notwithstanding, there was the issue of His people's free will. Would these victims cooperate with God's willingness to revive them?

When God extends a choice between life and death, what will His people choose? Ezekiel could only answer that God knew, but the fact that God mentioned life at all raised an engaging possibility. It sparked a glimmer of hope.

Indeed, no matter how hopeless a case may seem, the hope of Israel stands in the midst, mighty to save. And the secret of resurrection is to simply let Him be there for us.

CASE IN POINT:
Mary and Martha

Think of Mary and Martha, weeping over the loss of their brother, Lazarus. By the time Jesus got there it appeared to be completely hopeless. After all, this was no vision. Lazarus had been physically dead for four days. His body was already in a tomb. He was decomposing.

Still, Jesus promised that though Lazarus was dead, he would live again. It must have seemed impossible to Lazarus' sisters. Compassionately, Jesus explained:

> "*I am the resurrection, and the life; he who believes in Me shall live even if he dies.*"
>
> John 11:25

Think of so-called "hopeless cases" in your life, those desperately dry bones. A friend or family member may come to mind. You might feel like that hopeless case yourself. But as long as the God who will never leave us or forsake us is in our midst, anything is possible.

CASE IN POINT: William Cowper (conclusion)

For many, William Cowper must have seemed a hopeless case, given his life-long bouts with depression, doubt, and multiple suicide attempts. John Newton and Mary Unwin kept faithful watch over a life that seemed impossible to save. When Mary ultimately predeceased him, William was beyond consolation.

Still, God was in the midst.

Finally, William lay dying, not by his own hand, but of dropsy. His face was traced with the depression and anxiety that had characterized so much of his life.

In his weakened state, neither spiritual nor emotional recovery seemed possible for William. Yet, more sources than it is reasonable to cite report that, in his very last hour, a dramatic transformation occurred.

Moments before William passed into eternity, a profound change was observed in William. He looked up. Radiance overtook gloom. Hope was reborn. Wonder lit in his eyes.

Clearly relieved, William watched what no one else could see. It was like a great veil had been lifted, as if suddenly, William saw the secret to life's great mystery, standing there to greet him. A surprised smile curling on his lips, William famously marveled, *"I am not shut out of heaven after all."*

And so it was that William Cowper released his final earthly breath, in complete and utter peace. Like William's inspired verse, God had worked *"in a mysterious way, His wonders to perform."*

How does this apply to me?

You may still be asking yourself what Ezekiel's experience, or even William Cowper's, has to do with you. Well, the Bible says that "*Jesus is the same yesterday, today, yes and forever*" (Hebrews 13:8). The same way that God commanded Ezekiel to speak life into those dry bones, and the same way that Jesus called Lazarus forth from the tomb, the Spirit of God still stands calling. He still wants to speak His words of life to and through you.

He always will.

It's just the way He is.

Forever.

Think about the dry bones in your life. Picture them. Call their names to mind (even if you are among them). Make note in your journal to support each one in prayer.

Now, hear God's question:

"*Can these bones live?*"

The answer is a resounding *yes!* Resurrection is possible.

Paul talked about the dead being raised in the context of the last trumpet, but read his words below from a fresh perspective. Consider the application they can have for dry bones even now, on earth, as we await that great day:

"Behold, I tell you a mystery; we shall not all sleep, but we shall all be changed, in a moment, in the twinkling of an eye, at the last trumpet; for the trumpet will sound, and the dead will be raised imperishable, and we shall be changed. For this perishable must put on the imperishable, and this mortal must put on immortality...then will come about the saying that is written, 'Death is swallowed up in victory.'"

I Corinthians 15:51–53, 54b

Raising the dry bones isn't about mustering up belief in ourselves or in anyone else's ability to turn things around for themselves. It's all about the supernatural power of God. It's about embracing the victory that has already been won by Jesus' death and resurrection. It's about filling our chests with the reviving breath that only the Holy Spirit can give us. Just like that mystery Paul talked about, it's that exchange of what is perishing for what is eternal.

The good news is, we don't have to wait for the physical resurrection of the dead to start living in the kingdom. Jesus said the kingdom was at hand. The spiritually dry and dead can be resurrected at any time, in a moment, starting in the here and now. It's a message of hope God has hidden in our hearts, embedded with a call to be messengers for Him.

Why does God use messengers?

It's a fair question to ask. Why did God ask Ezekiel to prophesy to the dry bones? It's not like God needed Ezekiel's help. He could have taken out the fallible middleman. He could have spoken directly. His voice could have thundered out of heaven.

But that's not what happened.

God chose to involve His creation. He asked a human being to speak those words of life for Him. He asked Ezekiel to prophesy. He appointed Mary Unwin and John Newton to speak words of life to William Cowper. He still involves us today.

The fact is, throughout the Scriptures, God demonstrated a pronounced pattern of engaging human mouthpieces. We mess up. We get things wrong sometimes. But for some reason, God still wants to use us.

By His Spirit, God gives His people words of life. He asks them to speak to dry bones. Those words are called prophecy. Sure, the Greek word for prophecy can involve foretelling, but it can also just as accurately describe the act of speaking to another person under the inspiration of the Holy Spirit.

Take another look at how God directed the prophet in Ezekiel 37:9-14. Once again, put yourself into Ezekiel's sandals. Whether you're alone or in a group, read that whole portion of the passage aloud with feeling.

God's Call to Prophesy

No matter what your stature within the body of Christ, consider God's call to prophesy. Open your ears to hear what inspired words He may give you for the slain, dry bones in your life (Isaiah 50:4–5).

"Wait a sec. I'm not a prophet," you say. "I'm no Ezekiel."

Fair enough. I'm no Ezekiel either. I'm certainly no spiritual giant. But still, the call to prophesy goes out widely, to be earnestly sought, above all other spiritual gifts:

> *"Pursue love, yet desire earnestly spiritual gifts, especially that you prophesy...But the one who prophesies speaks to men for edification, exhortation and consolation."*
>
> I Corinthians 14:1, 3

Maybe you've always thought of prophecy in terms of God unveiling the future, but more often it serves those other purposes Paul mentioned—to *edify*, *exhort*, and *console*. Look for examples of these three functions of prophecy that are right there in Ezekiel's passage. So, let's try not to get derailed by the foretelling aspects of prophecy. That's only one of the ways that this multifaceted gift can manifest.

Why are we talking about prophecy in this study? First, it's important to realize that Ezekiel's dry bones vision is a prophecy in and of itself, but additionally, it was infused with a command to prophesy to the dry bones (v. 4). Ezekiel was also commanded to prophesy to the breath, to breathe on the slain (v.9). For that reason, no study of this passage would be complete without considering this spiritual gift that Paul urged all believers to seek.

To be sure, there's a lot of confusion about what it is to prophesy. What is the essence of prophecy? Remember, Revelation 19:10 gives us that simple explanation when it says: "*the spirit of prophecy is the testimony of Jesus.*" Prophecy really can be as simple as giving an inspired testimony about Jesus.

God may not give you a vision like Ezekiel. Maybe you're not called to the office of prophet. You might not receive word-for-word messages. But when you testify God's truth about Jesus—when you speak those words of life the Holy Spirit gives you—you are fulfilling the spirit of prophecy.

You may be led to speak life into a person by applying specific Scriptures. Maybe the Spirit will give you just the words you need to help encourage, exhort, or comfort someone whose bones seem so dry that he or she is beyond earthly help. Perhaps you'll be inspired to share the testimony of what Jesus has done in your life. These are all words that breathe life into the dying. Spoken with the Spirit's inspiration, these words can even be instrumental in raising the dead.

So, yes, pursue love. And, out of that love for God and your brethren, earnestly desire to prophesy to the dry bones in your life. Reveal the secrets of the kingdom that God has entrusted to you.

Just like Ezekiel did, you can speak to those dry bones. You can tell them that God can and will open their graves. He will put His Spirit within anyone who sincerely turns to Him. When that happens, the power of death will be broken. They will take in His breath and rise to their feet. All heaven will celebrate the resurrected life that comes forth.

BONE SCAN:
Witness Testimony

Let's take one last look inside ourselves to conclude this study. Understanding that the spirit of prophecy is the testimony of Jesus, that this gift can be manifest through speaking inspired words of encouragement, exhortation, and consolation to the perishing, ask yourself these questions:

- *Have I earnestly sought the gift of prophecy? If not, am I willing to?*
  (I Corinthians 14:1, 3)

- *Do I study the Scriptures in preparation to rightly handle the Word of truth?*
  (II Timothy 2:15)

- *Do I actively desire to bring the inspired testimony of Jesus to the dry bones?*
  (Acts 4:18–20)

- *What steps can I take to make myself more available to speak life to the dry bones?*
  (I Timothy 4:14–16)

It's my prayer that over the course of this study, you've taken more than just an arm's length view of Ezekiel's vision and the call that goes along with it.

Maybe, as you've read about this vision, the Holy Spirit has stirred you. Perhaps you've felt Him moving upon your own heart, encouraging you to inhale His life-giving breath anew. He may be prompting you to speak to the dry bones in your life—to your neighbors, friends, and family. If so, will you pray this closing prayer with me?

Yes, Lord,

I am one of Your people. I am one of the dead You have resurrected from this valley of dry bones. Thank You for breathing new life into me. Thanks for watering me with Your Word. Thank You for being faithful to Your promise to put Your Holy Spirit in me.

Right now, I receive the breath of life You give to me anew. Fill me to overflowing every day as I wake. I will walk out life's great mystery with Your hand in mine.

Let me hear the sound of Your whispers, Lord. Going forward, I will make a special point to listen for You. I want to learn to recognize Your still, small voice, and I will wholeheartedly answer Your call.

Please, Lord. Inspire me to prophesy to the dry bones. Equip me to speak Your words of encouragement, exhortation, and comfort. I offer myself as Your mouthpiece to the slain, to the dry and disconnected. I will call the dead to new life. I will walk in the Spirit, in the testimony of Jesus. It's in His great name that I pray. Amen.

Notes & Inspiration

"*Behold, I will open your graves and cause you to come up out of your graves, My People...and I will put my Spirit within you, and you will come to life.*"

Ezekiel 37:12, 14

About the Author

SUSAN ROHRER is an honor graduate of James Madison University where she enjoyed studying Art and Communications. Thereafter, she married in her native state of Virginia.

As a professional writer, producer, and director of redemptive entertainment, Rohrer's credits in one or more of these capacities include: an adaptation of *God's Trombones;* 100 episodes of the television drama series *Another Life;* Humanitas Prize finalist & Emmy winner *Never Say Goodbye;* Emmy nominees *Terrible Things My Mother Told Me* and *The Emancipation of Lizzie Stern;* anthology *No Earthly Reason;* NAACP Image Award triple nominee *Mother's Day;* AWRT Public Service Award winner (given for responsibly addressing the issue of teen sexual harassment) *Sexual Considerations;* comedy series *Sweet Valley High;* television movies *Book of Days* and *Another Pretty Face;* Emmy nominee & Humanitas Prize finalist *If I Die Before I Wake;* as well as Film Advisory Board & Christopher Award winner *About Sarah.*

Rohrer is also the author of THE HOLY SPIRIT – SPIRITUAL GIFTS: Books 1, 2, and the accompanying WORKBOOK: *Listening Prayer Applications for Book 1.* Rohrer also authored nonfiction titles SECRETS OF THE DRY BONES: *Ezekiel 37:1–14: The Mystery of a Prophet's Vision;* IS GOD SAYING HE'S THE ONE? *Hearing from Heaven about That Man in Your Life;* SPLASH!*: Inspirational Quotations;* PURE IN HEART: *The Secret to Seeing God;* DOWNSIZING*: How Decluttering Graces Your Heart and Home;* and *HOLY SPIRIT WHISPERS: Hearing the Still Small Voice of God.*

In addition to many nonfiction books, Rohrer has authored numerous inspirational novels in her *Redeeming* fiction series, each adapted from her own original screenplays, including: *Merry's Christmas, Merry's Christmas Wedding, Virtually Mine, Bright*

Christmas, What Laurel Sees, Bridle My Heart, Gifted, and *Grace Dawns.* Rohrer's novel *The Beautiful World* is an adaptation of her screenplay based on Eleanor H. Porter's beloved classic book, *Just David.*

—*Soli Deo Gloria*

Nonfiction
BY SUSAN ROHRER

The Holy Spirit—Spiritual Gifts
Amazing Power for Everyday People: Book 1

The Holy Spirit—Spiritual Gifts Workbook
Listening Prayer Applications for Book 1

The Holy Spirit—Spiritual Gifts
Surprisingly Supernatural Service Gifts: Book 2

Holy Spirit Whispers
Hearing God's Still, Small Voice

Is God Saying He's the One?
Hearing from Heaven about That Man in Your Life

Pure in Heart
The Secret to Seeing God

Splash!
Inspirational Quotations

Healer of My Soul
Through Deep Waters with Jesus
(by Lucinda Russell and Susan Rohrer)

Redeeming Fiction

BY SUSAN ROHRER

Merry's Christmas

Merry's Christmas Wedding

Bright Christmas

Virtually Mine

Bridle My Heart

What Laurel Sees

Gifted

Grace Dawns

The Beautiful World

A Final Note
Before We Say Goodbye

Dear Reader,

Thanks so much for the time we've spent together as you've read this book. I hope you've found it as meaningful to study as it was for me to prepare it.

Would you kindly consider posting a quick review? You'll get to share your reading experience with family, friends, and other readers across the world. And I'll truly appreciate your feedback.

Gratefully,
Susan Rohrer

Made in United States
North Haven, CT
08 February 2022

15846611R00075